Victor J. Kean

NEW LIGHT ON OLD MYSTERIES

EFSTATHIADIS
GROUP

Efstathiadis Group S.A.
Agiou Athanasiou Street,
GR - 145 65 Anixi, Attikis

ISBN 960 226 226 5

© Efstathiadis Group S.A. 1993

Printed and bound in Greece by Efstathiadis Group S.A.

To Stella

Contents

List of Illustrations

Fig. 1. Map of Rhodes.

10

Foreword

For all the many visitors to Rhodes, the island offers endless hours of sunshine and beautiful beach facilities against a historical background. The grey walls of the Old City stand massive and silent, waiting to be explored.

For the island is full of interest and mystery which can intrigue the visitor, making one's stay even more unforgettable.

Why did Julius Caesar and Mark Antony travel to the island of Rhodes? What brought the Queen of Sheba and the beautiful Helen of Troy so far to climb the steep steps up to the acropolis at Lindos?

Where stood the giant Colossus, one of the Ancient Seven Wonders of the World? When and where did Aphrodite come ashore on the island of Rhodes?

And what became of the School of Rhetoric and the ancient observatory where Hipparchus observed the heavens?

Why do the butterflies always remain in their unique valley each year?.... What ailments did the 'miracle waters' of Kallithea seek to cure?... And how did the Knights manage to storm the heights of Mt. Phileremo?

In searching out the answers to these mysteries, one

will discover many places off the normal tourist route. Long, unspoilt beaches where no other footsteps mark the smooth sand. Small tavernas hidden in tiny coves. Groves of olive trees that provide shade from the heat of the day. Mountain villages where the old Greek-style hospitality still prevails.

All will provide the reader with unforgettable memories of the lovely island of Rhodes.

Fig. 2. The Colossus of Rhodes.

·1 The Colossus of Rhodes

Having withstood the long siege of Demetrios in 304 B.C. the people of Rhodes celebrated their successful resistance by commissioning the sculptor, Chares of Lindos to produce a statue worthy of their efforts.

This enormous figure of Helios - the Sun God, which took twelve years to complete was cast in bronze. It was built piece by piece, working upwards from the feet until it stood eighty cubits high. Various sources give the height as between 31m. and 38m.

What is known for certain, is that the statue became one of the Seven Wonders of the World during the 56 years that it remained standing. Chares was paid some 300 talents; the proceeds from the sale of the great siege engines with which Demetrios had tried to breach the walls of the city.

After the destruction of the statue which resulted from the earthquake of 224 B.C. the islanders consulted the Oracle at Delphi. They were warned by the Oracle not to re-build the statue.

The popular belief that the statue straddled the entrance to the harbour was based on a mis-interpretation of the inscription which was around its base. However, this is how the statue is usually depicted (Fig. 2).

The broken pieces of the Colossus lay for many years where it had fallen, which allowed the populace to examine the hollow bronze castings.

Evidence that it was sold for scrap in 653 A.D. rules out the idea that it stood poised above the sea. Ancient records referring to a church called St. Johannes Colossensis suggests that the statue stood on land within the walled city.

Plate A. The Kneeling Aphrodite (1st Century B.C.).

2   Aphrodite - Goddess of Love

Born in the sea, the Goddess of Love emerged from the delicate foam off the island of Kythera, north of Crete. At least, that is one of the legends that surround this deity.

Her emergence from the waves has been portrayed in many works of art, both in paintings and in sculpture. Countless temples were built in her honour throughout the Mediterranean.

In 1912, whilst clearing the site of some old buildings in Rhodes Town, workmen discovered the statue of the Kneeling Aphrodite which has been dated to the 1st. Century B.C. (Plate A). The Goddess is shown streaming out her hair in the warmth of the sun to dry her wet tresses.

Some seventeen years later, fishermen hauling in their nets as they approached the quayside of Rhodes harbour, were startled to find the smooth marble figure of another statue of the Goddess entangled in their nets. Dated to the 3rd. Century B.C. this somewhat forlorn figure became known as the Marine Venus - the Roman name for Aphrodite. After its long immersion in the sea and the effect of the pounding waves, the Marine Venus bears the traces of her ordeal. She now rests with her younger sister in the quiet tranquillity of the Archaeological Museum.

The remains of the Temple of Aphrodite (3rd. Cent.) can be seen in Platia Symis (Arsenal Square) as one enters the Walled City from Symi Gate. It is possible that the Marine Venus was originally displayed in the Temple and had been taken aboard a Roman ship prior to its illegal shipment to Rome. It is known that many of these ships, over-laden and unstable, floundered and sank with their treasures on the voyage through the Mediterranean.

Plate B. Ancient Stadium of Rhodes.

3 Ancient Stadium of Rhodes

The ancient stadium stands in the south-west corner of the city. Built into a natural hollow, the rows of empty seats stare silently down at the deserted arena (Plate B). Though much of the stadium has been reconstructed, some of the tiers of seats are original. Over two thousand years ago, local athletes trained on this ground for the Olympic Games held every four years on the Peloponnese.

The shortest race was of one length and was known as the 'stade' or 'stadion'. The two length race, the 'diadulos' and the twenty length race, the 'dolichos' both used posts at the limit of each lap though these are now lost. The runners, exclusively male, were naked with the exception of the athletes in the foot race for men carrying shields and wearing helmets.

Of the local athletes, the most famous was Diagoros who stood almost 2m. tall and excelled in boxing. In the Games of 464 B.C. he was crowned the Victor. An achievement which he repeated at the Isthmic, Nemean and Pythian Games. Such was his fame throughout Rhodes and the whole of the Greek world that the poet Pindar wrote a hymn to his prowess. It is said that the hymn was written on a pillar of marble, with the letters in-filled with gold. The pillar was erected in the Temple sanctuary of the Lindian Athene at Lindos (See Section 12). The success of Diagoros was repeated by his two sons, Damagetos and Akousilaos in the years 452 and 448 B.C.

Visitors to the stadium will notice the much restored square-shaped theatre which is possibly the site of the famous School of Rhetoric which was held on Rhodes and attracted many well known personalities from Ancient Rome.

Coats of Arms
of the
Grand Masters

1310 **1319**

foulques de Villaret
(PROVENCE)

1319 **1346**

Helion de Villeneuve
(PROVENCE)

Knights of St John of Jerusalem

1346 **1353**

Dieudonne de Gozon
(PROVENCE)

1354 **1355**

Pierre de Corneillan
(PROVENCE)

Figs 3-22. Coats of Arms of the Grand Masters.

4   Knights of St. John of Jerusalem

It was almost the end of August in the year 1307 when the small flotilla consisting of two galleys and four smaller craft sailed down the east coast of Rhodes. Aboard the vessels were a vanguard of the Knights of St. John and supporting foot soldiers. They had sailed from Cyprus with the agreement of the Geonese Admiral Vignoli, to occupy and rule the island of Rhodes. The Byzantine forces already in occupation were determined to resist this invasion.

In a bold attempt to take the island by bluff, the Knights had previously sailed straight into the harbour of Rhodes, hoping that the mere sight of such determined and feared fighting men would persuade the Byzantines to lay down their arms without any bloodshed. It was not to be. They were greeted by a few well placed cannon shots across their bows. The flotilla was forced to sail out of range and head south down the coast.

Coming in sight of the ancient acropolis at Lindos upon which the Temple complex could be clearly seen, the flotilla turned into the bay of Pharaklos (Hariki). Here they dropped anchor beneath the watchful eyes of the Byzantine forces. Lining the walls of the castle which

1355   1365

Roger de Pins
(PROVENCE)

1365   1374

Raymond Berange
(PROVENCE)

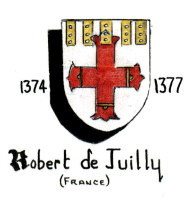

1374   1377

Robert de Juilly
(FRANCE)

1377   1396

Ferdinand d'Heredia
(SPAIN)

1396   142

Philibert de Naillac
(FRANCE)

stands on the northern escarpment, their enemy waited for them to disembark.

There is no record as to exactly how long the Knights waited on their cramped ships. When they did finally disembark their strength would have been accurately assessed by their enemy.

The storming of the Byzantine castle at Pharaklos and its eventual capture would not have been achieved without some loss of life. Thus this small force was further reduced.

It was now the end of September. Three months had passed since the 35 Knights and two hundred foot soldiers had left the island of Cyprus. Though they were now in command of the castle at Pharaklos the reduced force had no other successes to their credit. The Knights were aware that in order to capture the supreme prize of the city of Rhodes, they must first eliminate the Byzantine force entrenched on the top of Mount Phileremo.

Whilst repairing and strengthening the fortified walls of Pharaklos, the Knights sent out scouts to assess the strength of the Byzantine garrison on the other side of the island.

Such was the commanding view of the surrounding countryside enjoyed by the occupiers of Phileremo, that any movement of a large body of men would have been easily detected. Furthermore, the narrow tracks which wound up the mountain slopes were steep and twisting, thus preventing any quick advances. The scouts would have also discovered that extra guards had been posted about the summit.

Under cover of darkness, the Knights of St. John filtered through the countryside as they approached the

1421   1437

Antoine Fluvian
(Spain)

1437   1454

Jean de Lastic
(Auvergne)

1454   1461

Jacques de Milly
(Auvergne)

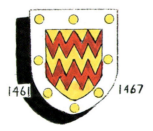

1461   1467

Raymond Zacosta
(Spain)

1467   1476

Giovanni B. degl. Orsini
(Italy)

mountain and slowly climbed upwards towards the Byzantine fortifications. Clad in their light chain - mail armour with the striking red background to the simple white cross, the Knights huddled together on the hillside.

Aware that a frontal assault was bound to fail, the Knights used guile and intelligence where other tactics seemed less hopeful. With the aid of a Greek servant who was in the pay of the Byzantines, the Knights were shown how to enter the tightly guarded compound without detection.

In the quiet hours between midnight and dawn, when even the best trained guards are less alert than usual, the Knights moved quietly through the Byzantine lines. Most of the force was well inside the enemy compound before the alarm was raised. Thus the Knights exploited the element of surprise to its full and devastating effect.

The Knights overran the compound, ruthlessly slaughtering all who opposed them. The Byzantine commander and his officers sought sanctuary in their chapel, leaving their Turkish mercenaries to the mercy of the Knights.

Over the next two years, the Knights were reinforced from Cyprus, but the Byzantine forces continued to retain their hold on the city of Rhodes. Not until August 1309 when the Knights displayed an enormous fleet of fighting ships off the coast did the beleaguered Byzantine army agree to surrender.

The Knights sailed triumphantly into the small northern harbour (Mandraki), which would have been difficult under any other circumstances to capture by a sea-borne assault. With banners flying they came ashore, the familar white cross of St. John against its red

1476   1505

Pierre d'Aubusson
(Auvergne)

1505   151

Aimerie d'Ambois
(France)

1512   1513

Guy de Blanchefort
(Auvergne)

1513   1521

Fabrizio del Carretto
(Italy)

1521   15

Ph. Villiers de l'Isle Ad.
(France)

32

background and the personal flag of Foulques de Villaret fluttering at the mast heads (Fig. 3). It was the beginning of the Knight's domination of the island of Rhodes and many of the smaller island which lay to the north west. The population of Rhodes benefited from the presence of the Knights who were able to ensure the safety of the Rhodian merchant ships against attacks from the Turks. Thus trade was able to flourish again.

Over the next two hundred years the Knights strengthened the walls of their castle and the city. The numerous coats - of - arms which can be seen at various places around the walls commemorates this work.

A truly international body, the Knights were divided into separate 'tongues' according to their language. They lived in 'Inns' which they shared with their comrades. France, Provence and Auvergne were each a separate Inn, giving the French greater voting power. The English, German, Italian and Spanish were also separately housed. The Spanish tongue eventually separating into the Inns of Castille and Aragon. Each separate tongue had a specific section of the outer wall to secure (Fig. 23). There was to be no misunderstandings due to language difficulties during the heat of battle. Under successive Grand Masters who took up residence in the Grand Master's Palace, the Knights continued to care for the sick, crippled and infirm. It was from this practise that their name, the 'Hospitallers' originated.

In 1444, the 600 Knights supported by 5000 Rhodian mercenaries withstood a seige by the Sultan of Egypt whilst under the command of Grand Master Jean de Lastic of Auvergne. Some 36 years later, the city was to withstand another seige. Under the leadership of

Mohammed II (The Conqueror), hoardes of screaming infidels attempted to storm the battlements only to be beaten back time and time again. This onslaught did much damage to the walls of the citadel. Then, before repair work could be started, a massive earthquake wreaked havoc with the fortifications. Under the energetic leadership of Pierre d' Aubusson (1476-1503) much rebuilding of the city and its wall was carried out. Thus the visitor will today find many instances of his particular coat-of-arms at various parts of the wall (Fig. 18).

Finally in 1522 after a seige lasting six months, during which time Sultan Suleimain II with 150,000 troops had cut off all vital supplies from reaching the Citadel, the Knights of the Order were forced to board their ships and depart from Rhodes for all time.

1. NAILLAC TOWER
2. FISHERMANS GATE
3. ST. CATHERINE'S GATE
4. ITALIAN TOWER
5. KOSKINOU GATE
6. ST. MARY'S TOWER
7. SPANISH TOWER
8. ST. GEORGE'S TOWER
9. AMBOISE TOWER
10. ST. ANTONY'S GATE
11. ST. PETER'S TOWER
12. TREBUC TOWER
13. WINDMILL TOWER
14. PALACE
15. HOSPITAL
16. STREET OF KNIGHTS

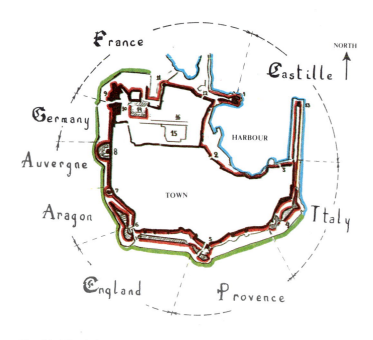

Fig. 23. The defensive posts of the Knights.

5   Citadel of Rhodes - 1522 A.D.

The fortified walled city of Rhodes is unique throughout Europe; its immensely thick walls were continually strengthened to withstand onslaught from without and to protect the harbours and thus ensure the vital lines of supply.

Inside the walled Citadel can be seen the Palace of Grand Masters, the Arsenal and the Knight's Hospital, now serving as the Archaeological Museum.

Entering through Freedom Gate from Mandraki Harbour one arrives in Arsenal Square (Platia Symis). Immediately opposite are the remains of the Temple of Aphrodite (3rd. Cent. B.C.). Walking up the street towards Platia Argyro one is surrounded by medieval buildings.

The Inn of England which was built in 1483 was destroyed by fire in the middle of the 19th Century. It was rebuilt in a faithful reproduction of the original and stands on the east side of the square opposite the Hospital (Arch. Museum). The English Knights were given one of the most vulnerable sections of the wall to defend between St. Mary's Tower (6) and Koskinou - St. John's Gate (5).

Fig. 24. Knight of the Order of St. John.

The French Knights who could muster the largest contingent of fighting men, defended the long section of outer wall of the Citadel between Amboise Tower (9) and the Naillac Tower (1).

The Inn of the tongue of Auvergne, one of the separate French tongues, stands behind the ancient Temple ruins. The cannon balls which lie outside the Inn date back to 1522 A.D. The Knights from Auvergne were responsible for defending the stretch of wall between St. George's Tower (8) and the Spanish Tower (7).

The Knights from Provence, whose Inn can be seen just beyond the arch spanning the famous 'Street of Knights', guarded the section of the outer wall between Koskinou Gate (5) and the Italian Tower (4).

The Spanish Knights who were eventually separated into the tongues of Aragon and Castille were quartered in their Inn which lies on the left hand side almost at the top of the Street of Knights. Aragon held the defensive post between St. Mary's Tower (6) and the Spanish Tower (7), whilst the tongue of Castille defended the War Harbour.

The Inn of Italy with the coat - of - arms of Fabrizo del Carretto above its doors is on the right hand side of the Street of Knights. The Round Tower of Italy, known also as Carretto's Tower (4) marks the beginnings of the sections of wall under the control of the Italian Knights. It extends to St. Catherine's Gate.

The Knights of Germany who defended the outer wall between the towers of St. George (8) and Amboise (9), a comparatively small section of the wall in keeping with their numbers, were housed in the Inn of Germany. This Inn vanished in the tremendous explosion of 1856 which also destroyed the Church of St. John and the Palace of the Grand Masters.

The Knight's Hospital which housed the sick, wounded and infirm on the first floor, reminds us that the 'Hospitallers' as they were known, always considered that caring for the sick was one of the primary aims of their Order. The heap of cannonballs which can be seen in the inner courtyard, date back to the seige of 305 B.C. when they were used in the massive catapults of Demetrios.

An early start is recommended in order to be able to walk up the Street of Knights and to be able to view it when quiet and deserted. It is said that beneath the arch which spans the street, the sharp tap of horse's hooves on cobbles can still be heard on certain days.

In those turbulent times, only the Knights of the Order were permitted inside the Inner Citadel at night. One can imagine the colourful scenes inside the various Inns of these dedicated men serving so far from their native countries.

The view over Mandraki Harbour from the Grand Master's Palace is unsurpassed, particularly at the start of the day.

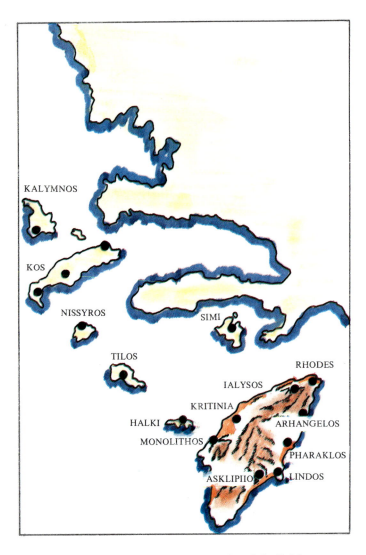

Fig. 25. Rhodes and the outer islands - Castles of the Knights.

6 The Castles of Rhodes and the Outer Islands

The Knights of the Order of St. John of Jerusalem, having captured the island of Rhodes in 1308 after their forced evacuation of Cyprus, remained for the next 200 years. During this period they strengthened the existing castle walls and built new fortifications in order to defend their position.

Apart from the fortified walls of the Citadel, a chain of other castles was established through the rest of the island. A communication system consisting of warning beacons and bonfires, smoke signals and even the use of homing pigeons was constantly maintained.

Castle walls still exist at Archangelos some 35 km down the eastern coast and further south at Haraki (Pharaklos) the remains of the Byzantine castle, which was the first to be captured by the Knights on their arrival, crown the heights overlooking the bay.

From this vantage point the fortified walls and castle of Lindos can be clearly seen. Here again the Knights strengthened the Byzantine castle which they captured after much fighting. In 1317 A.D. the Knights were forced to eject their own Grand Master Foulques de Villaret from Lindos.

Further south, outside the mountain village of Asklipion which lies inland, another castle continued the chain of command.

On the western side of the island, the fortified walls and castle at Phileremos (Ialysos) stand amongst the far older remains on this unique site.

Outside Kritina, some 52 km down the coastal road that runs down the west coast of the island, stands the well-preserved Castle of Kritina, built towards the end of the Knight's stay on Rhodes.

One of the most impressive castles on Rhodes is Monolithos (Grk. single rock). It was built some 240m. above the sea commanding the movements of shipping to the nearby islands of Alimina and Halki. With only one entrance gate at the top of open steps, Monolithos Castle could not be easily attacked. From its lofty battlements, magnificent views of the surrounding ocean and the distant islands can be enjoyed.

Though stretches of the sea wall of the castle of Halki have slipped down into the sea below, the entrance gate with its distinctive French coat - of - arms (Plate M) still remains visible and can be reached after a stiff climb. The tiny chapel of the Knights can be found within the castle walls.

The castles on the islands of Alimnia and Halki were the first links in the communication chain which reached out from the island of Rhodes. This chain of command continued with castles on Tilos, Nisyros, Kos, Kalymnos and Leros. An almost straight line across the Aegean (Fig 25). Further east, the castle on the island of Symi gave the Knights protection in that quarter of their domain.

Plate C. Mycenaean ceramics from Trianda.

7 Minoan settlement at Trianda

The excavated site of the Minoan settlement at the village of Trianda on the west coast of the island are all that remains of the influx of these immigrant people from the island of Crete.

Our sparse knowledge of these gentle invaders is enriched by the study of the three distinctive phases of building development which existed at Trianda.

The first phase, known to the excavators as Trianda I contained pottery which was readily datable to the Late Minoan period (LM IA). Thus it was established that the original arrivals came ashore around 1550-1500 B.C.

The next building phase (Trianda IIA) was found to contain ceramics similar to those found at Knossos, Crete and were dated to the period 1500-1450 B.C. (LMIB). In addition to these were found numerous pottery shards of Mycenaean type IIA. The findings of these two different ceramic styles indicated that this small Minoan settlement was able to maintain trade with both Crete and the Peloponnese (Plate C).

Evidence of a massive earthquake, the effects of which caused much structural damage to the settlement and the determined rebuilding which followed is a silent witness to the tenacity of the Minoans. This final building phase contained pottery from the period around 1425 B.C. It is similar in style to that of Knossos (LMII). The Minoan settlement was finally destroyed around 1410 B.C. probably by the warring Mycenaeans who had overwhelmed Crete following the volcanic eruption of Thera (Santorini).

The remains of the settlement lie some 100 m. from the junction with the main coastal road at Trianda, on the right hand side of the road leading to the sea. After some deterioration at the site due to excessive flooding, it was recently decided to infill the settlement with sand.

Plate D. Entrance Walk at Ialysos.

8   Ialysos - Crown of Mount Phileremo

Climbing inland from Trianda, the road towards Ialysos winds its way higher and higher as it approaches Mount Phileremo. Standing some 267 m. above sea level the triangular-shaped plateau offers the visitor an ancient time-capsule where the remains of Greek temples can be seen amongst Byzantine and other medieval buildings in a site unequalled on the island.

Before reaching this intriguing site whose history can be traced back to the Mycenaean Age (1410 B.C.) pause at one of the wide hairpin bends that mark the stiff climb to the summit and enjoy the magnificent views of the northern point of the island towards the City of Rhodes.

Like a natural carpet at your feet, the fields and plantations of the farms reflect the colour and harmony of nature's glory. Here in the heat of the summer, strong heady aromas of pine and jasmine mingle with oleander and roses in rich delight. Small wonder that men throughout the ages have made their way to this chosen place and built shrines, temples, churches and monasteries amongst the tall trees which embrace the hillside.

The avenue of cypress trees with its stepped path leads towards the summit (Plate D). An early Christian basilica has been built partly over the Temple of Athene Polias, adjacent to a Byzantine church which in turn became the entrance to the Chapel of the Knights. A restored medieval monastery and Byzantine castle completes the complex.

South of the square, a path leads down the side of the hill to a Doric (4th Cent.) fountain house where fresh water from the mountain side flowed through lion - headed spouts. Beneath the cool shade of the plane tree which shelters the fountain from the sun, further views of the surrounding countryside can be obtained.

Ialysos which was known in ancient times as "Achaia" reflects man's continual appreciation of places of unique beauty and tranquillity.

Plate 5. The Valley of Butterflies

9   Valley of Butterflies

Turning inland at the village of Soroni, 24 km from Rhodes Town and heading towards Dimilia, leads to the village of Petaloudes (Grk. butterflies). Here can be found the heavily wooded valley known throughout the Mediterranean as the 'Valley of Butterflies' (Plate E).

From the middle of June to the middle of September, the valley hums with the beat of butterfly wings. A delightful path winds through the valley over rustic bridges and past scenic waterfalls, providing a relaxing experience of the wonders of nature (Plate F). Even outside the season, the walk through the valley is well worth enjoying.

The main family of butterflies to be found is 'Callimorpha quadripunctaria', so called from the four distinctive markings on its wings (Plate G). The Quadrina butterflies with their multicoloured wings of red, white, black and brown are able to hide from view by camouflaging themselves with wings folded against the trunks of the trees. The sound of blown whistles send the butterflies into the air with a startling burst of vivid colour, as guides steer parties of visitors through the valley.

Plate F. Rustic bridges through the valley.

Plate G. Callimorpha quadripunctaria.

The abundance of storax trees from which a resin is obtained, attracts the butterflies with its heady fragrance. The resin is used to produce incence for the churches and, in the heat of the summer, can be readily detected in the air.

It is this attractive aroma which ensures that, each year for our constant delight, the butterflies will be found in the valley.

Fig. 26. Ancient Kamiros - Past and Present.

10   Ancient Kamiros

Though the remains of the ancient city of Kamiros bear the ravages of time, the site still retains its fascination. The main street, either side of which stood the residential quarters and the religious areas, leads through the centre of the city towards the acropolis. It is from the acropolis that one can enjoy a panoramic view of the city and the sea beyond.

Across the acropolis, a magnificent Doric stoa once stretched along the 200 m. wide plateau (Fig. 26). Consisting of two rows of columns supporting an angled roof, the stoa contained a series of shops or living quarters. Attempts to re-erect six of the columns was sadly frustrated when they toppled during a violent storm in 1962.

Prior to the building of the stoa, two large water cisterns stored rainwater for the eventual supply to the townspeople. Traces of the waterproof coating which was applied to the walls to prevent seepage can still be seen today. The two flights of steps leading down into the bottom of the cistern were to aid cleaning. Two movable conical shaped lids acted as valves to regulate the flow of water into the town. When the stoa was built over the cisterns, a series of 16 wells with inter-connections were sunk into the ground. Clay pipes and conduits, the remains of which can still be found amongst the houses distributed the precious rain water. Thus, even in the rain free summer months of 3000 years ago, the citizens of Kamiros enjoyed their supply of drinking water.

Numerous temples and religious shrines stood in the open spaces adjacent to the houses. The main street was flanked with large statues which stood on stone bases some of which still remain. These included the torso of a Kouros (6th. Cent. B.C.) which can be seen in the Archaeological Museum in Rhodes along with the other removable finds from Kamiros. These also include examples of Kamiros coinage which depicted a fig leaf as the symbol of the city. Many fine quality vases were also unearthed and are now on display in Room Z of the Museum.

Amongst the remains of the houses can be found a smoke-blackened brazier and part of an elementary sundial with carefully inscribed divisions.

Though severely damaged by the great earthquake of 226 B.C. the city of Kamiros continued to be inhabited down through the ages.

The excavations at Kamiros which were begun in 1852 by Biliotri and Salzmann, were continued in 1928 by other Italian archaeologists.

Plate H. Kallithea Spa.

11   Kallithea - Spa of Miracle Waters

The healing power of the waters of Kallithea spa were known to the great Hippocrates - the father of modern medicine who was born on the island of Kos.

People seeking relief from such ailments as arthritis, liver and kidney problems and various other forms of indigestion made the journey to Kallithea from all parts of the Mediterranean. In addition to drinking the so-called 'miracle' water, total immersion was also practised.

Situated some 10 km from the city of Rhodes on the eastern side of the island, the spa was refurbished under the orders of the Italian dictator, Mussolini. He envisaged the island as his own personal retreat during the time when the island was under Italian control.

Though somewhat faded now with the passage of time, the buildings which stand at the head of a picturesque cove set amongst pine trees, still glow in Florentine blue and pink colours (Plate H).

Beneath the domed structure at the centre of the complex, the 'miracle' water was pumped high through a decorative fountain and then cascaded down into a surrounding basin. Alcoves and niches built into the

Plate I. Pergola at Kallithea.

Plate J. Dome of Spa.

walls of the surrounding buildings provided private shelters and sun-bathing facilities for the afflicted. Plans to renovate the complex and regenerate the water are at present under consideration.

Beyond the spa through the pine trees, the beach alongside the sea is considered by many to be one of the best beaches on the island and is highly recommended.

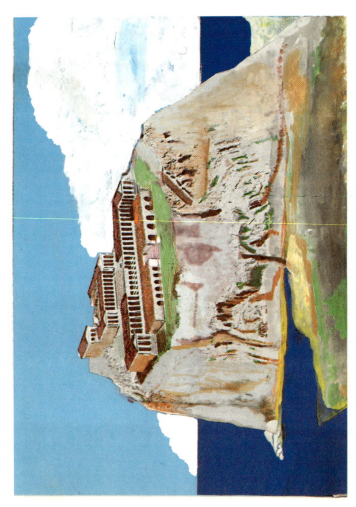

Fig. 27. Temple complex of the Lindian Athene - Lindos.

12   Lindos - Shrine of the Lindian Athene

High on the ancient acropolis known as Lindos, stands the temple of the Lindian Athene. For thousands of years, the shrine was the most revered centre in the Mediterranean, attracting to the island many of the famous persons in history.

Helen of Troy and the Queen of Sheba visited Rhodes in order to pay homage at the shrine, as did Ptolemy I and Amassis from Ancient Egypt. From the Roman Empire came Mark Antony, Julius Caesar, Pompey, Brutus and Cicero. Alexander the Great and Philip V also climbed the steep and narrow path that led up to the temple complex.

Prior to the arrival of the Byzantines, the acropolis was not fortified and stood in splendid view for miles around with its red roofs and gleaming columns (Figure 27). The area not occupied by buildings was covered with olive trees, amongst which stood numerous statues. Entering the complex by climbing the narrow stairway, the visitor crossed to the wide steps of the lower patio. From here one could look up through the columns of the wide stoa on the next level. Once on the patio and crossing to the stoa, reveals another flight of steps rising further in the front of the Propylaeum. Reaching this level, one passed between the columns and across the courtyard to the small Temple of the Athene which stood in the corner of the triangular - shaped plateau.

Inside the Doric Temple stood the statue of the Lindian Athene, fashioned in gold - covered wood with a marble head crowned in golden wreaths, the statue stood on a raised dias. The marble fingers of her left hand rested lightly on a shield, whilst in her right hand she held a phial of nectar.

Fig. 28. Bay of Lardos.

13   Keskinto - Site of an Ancient Observatory

Visitors to the island of Rhodes can join a modern day quest to find the site of the ancient observatory at Keskinto. The first hurdle to be surmounted is to accurately locate the long overgrown location of Keskinto.

No reference to Keskinto will be found on any of the modern maps available for purchase.

Keskinto was situated some 3 kms. south of the present town of Lardos, south-west of Lindos. The ancient astronomers sought a favourable site close to the nominal latitude (36°) of the island and where they also would have an unobstructed view of the eastern horizon (Fig. 28). Thus they would be able to observe the morning sunrise, an essential natural time-keeper in the days before mechanical devices.

Keskinto (Ancient Lardos) stood in a narrow, fertile plain with higher ground to the south which overlooks the Bay of Lardos with its wide, unspoilt beaches. From here the heavens could be studied and the risings and settings of the fixed stars recorded. The planets, known to the ancients as the 'wanderers' were also studied in depth.

Hipparchus observed the lunar eclipse on Jan 27th

141 B.C. from the island of Rhodes and again in August 128 B.C. In May and June 127 B.C. he made other lunar observations from the island. The second part of his 'Commentary to Aratus' deals with the risings and settings of the fixed stars, as seen from the horizon of Rhodes.

Around 100 B.C. an astronomer, thought by some to have been Attalus of Rhodes, developed a theory concerning the planets: Mercury, Mars, Jupiter and Saturn. His conclusions were carefully inscribed on a stone stele which was erected at Keskinto. It referred to the planets in their correct order from the Sun. It contained the first recorded reference to a circle being divided into 360 degrees. It refers to half degrees as 'points'. The bulk of the text was inscribed in 8 mm. high letters in Ancient Greek script. There are three groups of text, each with four lines. Each line refers to an astronomical parameter which, according to O. Neugebauer is based on the assumption that 29140 years contain an equal number of revolutions and phases for the outer planets.

The inscription ends with a line of 13 mm. high letters interpreted as ... 'a Thanksgiving to the Gods'.

In 1893, the lower part of this inscribed stone was discovered by a worker from Lindos in the little valley of Keskinto. Though badly weathered, impressions taken from the face of the stone reveal the astronomer's work.

The recovered fragment which measures $78 \times 31 \times 12$ cm now lies in the storage vaults of the Antikensammlung of the Staatliche Museum in East Berlin.

The upper part of this unique astronomical record in stone has yet to be found.

14   Embona - Village in the Mountains

The mountain village of Embona lies at 600 m. above sea level in the shadow of Mount Attavyros. The village can be reached by taking the minor road from Kritinia, or alternatively heading inland from Kalavarda and on through Salakos.

The village is surrounded by vineyards from which is produced the distinctive Embona wine. This wine is renowned all over the island and can be sampled at any of the tavernas in the district.

Far from the normal tourist route, the people of Embona still offer the old-style Greek hospitality to visitors. Overnight accomodation will also be offered to those wishing to stay longer.

The sharp eyes and nimble fingers of the old ladies, produce high-quality lace and embroidery which ranges from small handkerchiefs to full-size table cloths. All are offered at reasonable prices far below those of Rhodes city.

The Embona women dancers are appreciated throughout the Aegean and still dance on occasion in full traditional dress to the accompaniment of violin, bouzouki and drums. From August 6th until the end of the month, various dance festivals are held in the village.

The summit of Mount Attavyros stands some 1215 m. above sea level and can be reached after a stiff climb of about 2 hours by following the mountain path which begins just outside the village. Just below the peak, the few remains of the Hellenistic Temple to Zeus can be seen. It was to this small shrine that the islanders would make their way to pay homage to the Greek God of Heaven and Earth.

Plate K. The Tranquil Isle.

15   Halki - The Tranquil Isle

Lying off shore, some 10 km. to the west of the island of Rhodes, the small unspoilt island of Halki can be reached by either of two routes. It is regular port of call for the large passenger ships from Piraeus which sail through the Aegean linking Rhodes with the mainland. Halki can also be reached by arranging passage with one of the Captains of the two small caiques which ply daily between Kamiros Skala and Halki.

Approaching the island of Halki, the town which surrounds the harbour appears to house a large community (Plate K). This is not so. Many of the multi-coloured houses are abandoned and have remained empty for many years.

The sheltered harbour with its church, post office and three tavernas is the centre of the island's activity. The population barely exceeds 150; whilst the number of tourists who stay on Halki is extremely low.

As soon as the large ferry boat has departed, the quiet tranquillity of the island returns. A single road climbs between the houses from the harbour and crests the hill before dropping down to Potomas Bay with its narrow strip of sand. The shallow bay is an ideal, safe bathing

Plate L. Castle of the Knights.

Plate M. Coat-of-arms above Entrance.

place. A thriving taverna serves traditional Greek dishes. Local honey is also available.

The single hotel on the island is about to open for business and many rooms are on offer from the friendly inhabitants. A few modern rooms for rent overlook the bay.

The road continues past the sparse remains of an Athene temple and winds its way up between the hills. On one of the coastal peaks stands the remains of the Castle built between 1476-1505 (Plate L). Magnificent views across the sea to the islands of Alimnia and Rhodes can be obtained from the castle ramparts.

The single track road continues for another 2 Kms. before ending in a wide turning circle, though apart from one or two mopeds there are no motor vehicles on the island.

After the lively bustle of Rhodes City with its casinos and discos, the island of Halki sleeps in the past as the long summer afternoons lengthen into the quiet of the evening.

The evening meal at one of the harbour side tavernas where the local fishermen and their families meet in the old style is preceded by the evening promenade. An old Greek custom rarely seen nowadays.

At times of religious festivals, the young people of Halki make the long trek up through the mountains to the white walled chapel on the far end of the island. Here they stay overnight, enjoying the music and dancing which follows the service. Returning the following morning with much singing and natural gaiety, the islanders celebrate the festival with further dancing.

The lack of fresh water which has inhibited Halki's progress over the years is now resolved by the latest efforts of a team from U.N.E.S.C.O.

Victor J. Kean is a freelance writer specialising in archaeology, history and travel. The first of his archaeological works, "The Disk from Phaistos" was published in 1985 and was followed by the intriguing story of the "Antikythera Mechanism", the ancient Greek computer. Now he has written the second in a new series entitled "RHODES - New light on Old Mysteries" which provides a guide to the island's history and an introduction to some of the lesser known delights which await the visitor.

Also in this series:

1) Crete.
3) "Kerkyra" (Corfu).